The Art of Sugarcraft

CHOCOLATE

The Art of Sugarcraft

CHOCOLATE

PAT ASHBY

Special Preparation
for Photography
by Nicholas Lodge

Foreword Paddy Dunne
Series Editor Joyce Becker
Photography by Melvin Grey and Graham Tann

MEREHURST PRESS
LONDON

Published 1986 by Merehurst Press
5 Great James Street
London WC1N 3DA

ISBN 0 948075 09 0

Designed by Carole Perks
Editorial Assistant Suzanne Ellis
Further assistance provided by Trudie Ballantyne, Eleanor Field,
    Rachel Lalley and Sara Townshend
Cover photograph by Melvin Grey
Typeset by Filmset
Colour separation by Fotographics Ltd, London-Hong Kong
Printed by New Interlitho S.p.A., Milan

ACKNOWLEDGEMENTS
Pat Ashby would like to thank George, Susan and Justin Ashby and
Barbara Nayler for their help in the preparation of this book.

The publishers would like to thank the following companies for their
help in the preparation of this book:

Cuisena Cookware Limited
Guy, Paul and Company Limited, Unit B4, A1 Industrial Park,
    Little End Road, Eton Scoton, Cambridgeshire, PE19 3JH
Sugarflair Colours Limited
B.R. Mathews, 12 Gipsy Hill, London SE19 1NN
A Piece of Cake, 18 Upper High Street, Thame, Oxon, OX9 2XE
Elizabeth David Limited, 46 Bourne Street, London SW1 and at
    Covent Garden Kitchen Supplies, 3 North Row, The Market,
    London WC2
C.E.P. Moulds
McDougalls Kakebrand, Birling Road, Ashford, TN24 8BH
The Nestlé Company Ltd., St. George's House, Croydon, Surrey,
    CR9 1NR
Orchard Products, 49 Langdale Road, Hove, Sussex, BN3 4HR

Companion volumes:
The Art of Sugarcraft — **MARZIPAN**
The Art of Sugarcraft — **PIPING**
The Art of Sugarcraft — **SUGAR FLOWERS**

CONTENTS

FOREWORD

To many people, 'chocolate' brings to mind a picture of various bars, or of beautifully presented boxes of treats. In this book, the author, in a very artistic manner, presents some very attractive alternatives.

Creating items similar to those described and beautifully illustrated in this book requires the sugarcraft artist to follow precise instructions. By following the author's directions, even the beginner or someone with limited experience, will master the art of chocolate work, producing items with such a nice snap and good gloss that they, themselves, will glow with satisfaction.

As presentation is of immense importance, a study of the ideas presented by the author, plus a measure of imagination, will open up a new area in the world of sugarcraft.

Paddy Dunne
Technical advisor
Stewart & Arnold, Caxton

PAT ASHBY

Being a qualified teacher and
cake decorator with a unique
creative ability makes Pat Ashby
a popular sugarcraft artist, par-
ticularly in the areas of marzipan
modelling and chocolate work.

London-born Pat began to
study cake decorating at Brighton
Technical College, where she
became proficient in sugarcraft
techniques and obtained her
teacher's certificate.

A trip to Germany, where
every town has its marzipan
factory, gave Pat her interest in
this area of sugarart. Because
marzipan and chocolate are often
combined in decorating, she
became an expert in chocolate
work as well. She now teaches
these two subjects, as well as
other icing techniques and her

students win prizes at all of the sugarcraft exhibitions.

Pat herself prefers to judge competitions rather than enter them. She is a member of the Sugarcraft Guilds of Britain, America, Australia and South Africa, and she is in close contact with sugarcraft artists all over the world. In 1985, she co-authored FINISHING TOUCHES — THE ART OF CAKE DECORATING.

Pat Ashby now lives in Hove with her husband George, a retired engineer. They have three children.

NICHOLAS LODGE

Nicholas Lodge is one of the brightest lights in the young generation of sugarcraft artists. Although still in his early twenties, he already has an impressive collection of awards for his outstanding skills in the field of cake decoration.

Nicholas studied cake decoration at the National Bakery School, London, where he was awarded the prize for the best decoration student in his final year. He then worked in a bakery to gain practical experience before joining one of Britain's leading commercial cake decorating firms. As principle designer, Nicholas was responsible for producing cakes commissioned from leading stores and hotels. He also taught Australian and South African icing techniques.

He has taught sugarcraft to students at all levels, as well as demonstrating cake decorating and chocolate work in shops and department stores all over the UK. In addition, he has given short decorating courses in Singapore, Malaysia and Indonesia and Japan, with many overseas trips planned for the future.

CHOCOLATE — FOOD OF THE GODS

The first European lucky enough to taste chocolate was probably Hernán Cortés the explorer, who was given a cup of 'xocoatl' by Montezuma the Aztec emperor. The Aztecs considered the drink so glorious that it was served in golden goblets to members of the imperial family only. But it was a far cry from the comforting frothy drink we know. It was bitter, and served cold.

However, the cacao beans used to make the drink were also used as money by the Aztecs. Impressed by this, in 1528 Cortés took some of the beans back to his own king, Charles V of Spain. Charles V described chocolate as 'the divine drink that builds up resistance and fights fatigue'.

The Spanish explorers had also come across sugar in the New World and this was added to the chocolate, along with water and the drink was heated. Spices, such as vanilla and cinnamon, newly arrived from the West Indies, were included in some recipes and the drink became popular with the Spanish court. They kept the recipe a secret for nearly a hundred years, but gradually the reputation of the sweet delicious drink spread to other European courts and it became the drink one must serve a royal guest.

It was an enterprising French-man who opened the first shop in London selling solid chocolate for making the drink. Because of high import tax it was a luxury that only the wealthy could afford to drink. Chocolate houses serving hot chocolate were opened in London and other European capitals and these became the fashionable places in which to be seen. About 1700, the English began to add milk to the drink, and the vanilla and cinnamon were left out, making a blander drink. The Quakers

praised the new beverage as they thought hot chocolate might replace gin as a popular drink!

In the late eighteenth century Dutch and French chemists experimented with pressing the cacao beans to extract some of their fat — an amber liquid called cocoa butter. The solid mass which remained was crushed and sifted, producing cocoa powder. Later cocoa butter and sugar were added to ground beans and sweet (eating) chocolate was

born. In 1875 the Swiss introduced milk chocolate for eating. By this time, the high tax on imported cacao beans had been lifted and chocolate became a treat that all could afford and enjoy.

Throughout its long history chocolate has been considered special, not only for its taste but for its ability to give quick energy — due to its high carbohydrate level and the minute amount of caffein it contains. Blocks of chocolate are standard rations for hungry children and tired grown-ups, as well as astronauts and climbers of Everest.

In 1720 the cacao bean tree was given its scientific Latin name. The lovely name chosen was Theobroma — 'food of the gods'. From Montezuma to children devouring chocolate biscuits to the delights and decorations described in this book, chocolate is indeed a divine feast.

PRODUCING CHOCOLATE

Cacao beans grow only in tropical countries — Africa's west coast and Brazil are the main producers. Pods like small melons, which contain the beans, are harvested twice a year. They are split open and the beans are left to ferment in the blistering tropical sun for several days. During this time the white beans turn dark brown and begin to obtain their chocolaty flavour. They are dried and shipped in bags to the USA and Europe — the chocolatiers of the world. It takes one tree's yearly crop to make 450g (1lb) of cocoa.

At the chocolate factory, the cacao beans are cleaned, roasted and shelled. The roasting fills the air with chocolate's mouth-watering aroma. The beans are broken into large pieces called nibs and then these are ground, producing a rich brown liquid or paste called 'chocolate liquor' (although it has no alcoholic content). This liquor is the main ingredient for all chocolate products. Some of the liquor is hardened into moulds to form baking (bitter) chocolate but most is pressed to extract the cocoa butter. The resulting block, once the cocoa butter has been removed, is called 'press cake'. This is dried and sifted to make cocoa powder.

These three products — chocolate liquor, cocoa powder and cocoa butter — are combined to make all the different kinds of chocolate.

To make milk chocolate, the chocolate liquor is added to fluid or powdered milk and sugar. If cocoa butter and sugar only are used, with no chocolate liquor, white chocolate will result. Cocoa butter plus chocolate liquor and sugar makes the familiar sweet (eating) chocolate. If vegetable fat

is substituted for cocoa butter, the resulting baker's or compound chocolate cannot be legally sold as chocolate in most countries.

The mixtures are blended, spices and flavourings may be added, then the chocolate undergoes a long stirring or 'conching' period to make it smooth and creamy. After this, it is moulded into blocks and bars, wrapped and shipped to bakeries where it is used as an ingredient in cakes and biscuits, or sent straight to confectioneries.

WORKING WITH CHOCOLATE

There are two types of chocolate for use in sugarcraft — baker's chocolate and couverture. Baker's chocolate, also called compound chocolate, is much easier to work with, but does not have as good a flavour as couverture, which is the purest form of chocolate. Most of the chocolate work in this book can be done using either type of chocolate. In the few ideas where couverture is required, this is clearly stated. Both types are available in plain, milk and white forms.

Baker's chocolate

Baker's chocolate is available from most supermarkets and sugarcraft suppliers in slabs or buttons. It differs from couverture in that most of the cocoa butter has been removed and replaced with a vegetable fat, eliminating the need for tempering.

To melt baker's chocolate, place in the top of a double saucepan over hand hot water and stir until melted. Heat to a temperature of 38-43°C (100-110°F), or until completely smooth, if not using a thermometer. If the chocolate gets too hot it may have fat bloom — white streaks — when unmoulded. White sugar bloom may appear if the chocolate is too cool. Never allow steam or moisture to get in contact with the chocolate, or it will thicken and become unusable.

Baker's chocolate can be placed in the refrigerator after it has set to hasten contraction. Do not put couverture in the refrigerator or it may develop bloom.

Couverture

Chocolate work done with couverture will be smooth and glossy, and the flavour will be better than baker's chocolate. However, couverture has to be tempered before use. Couverture is available from sugarcraft suppliers and some specialist food shops. Most bars of dessert chocolate are made by a different process and are not suitable for chocolate work, so be sure that the chocolate you are using is pure couverture.

There are many different methods for tempering couverture, which involves heating and then cooling the chocolate to a precise temperature so that the

fat in the cocoa butter crystallizes. Well-tempered chocolate will have a high gloss and snap when set. A chocolate or clinical thermometer or sugar thermometer is necessary for tempering.

This method of tempering works for quantities up to 450g (1lb) of plain chocolate. Break the chocolate into small pieces and melt in the top of a double saucepan over simmering, not boiling, water. When the chocolate reaches 46°C (115°F), remove the pan from the hot water and place in a bowl of cold water. Stir until the chocolate cools to 27-28°C (80-82°F), then return to the pan of hot water and heat to 31°C (88°F), when the chocolate is tempered and ready for use. If tempering milk chocolate, the temperatures should be 1°C (2°F) lower at all stages.

Another method is to melt the chocolate in a double saucepan as above and heat to 46°C (115°F) for plain chocolate or 43°C (110°F) for milk. Pour two-thirds of the chocolate onto a cold marble slab and spread out with a palette knife. Work with a plastic scraper to bring the temperature down. The chocolate will begin to set at this point. Return it to the pan and reheat to 31°C (88°F) for plain or 29°C (84°F) for milk which will take a very short time. The chocolate is ready for use.

Chocolate which is not tempered correctly will not set well, and unmoulding will be difficult. There may also be a white or grey bloom on the surface.

EQUIPMENT

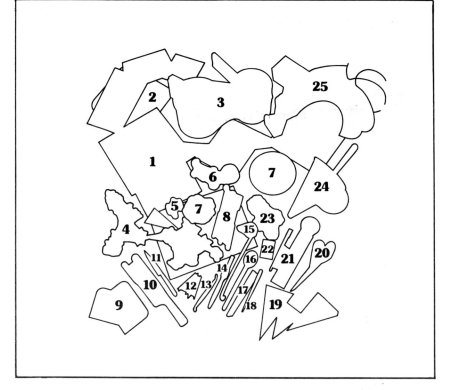

This is a selection of tools and equipment used for chocolate work. Most are ordinary kitchen or household items, while the more unusual tools are available from cake decorating shops and specialist suppliers.

1 Chocolate moulds
2 Baking tray
3 Double saucepans
4 Biscuit and pastry cutters
5 Petal dust for colouring
6 Paper and foil cases
7 Bowls for moulding
8 Dipping forks
9 Side scrapers
10 Palette knives
11 Sharp knife
12 Cocktail sticks
13 Ball tool
14 Pastry brush
15 Ladle
16 Wooden spoon
17 Paintbrushes
18 Scriber
19 Piping bags
20 Scissors
21 Chocolate and sugar thermometers
22 Glass-headed pins
23 Cotton wool
24 Chocolate funnel
25 Boxes and ribbons for packaging

RECIPES

Chocolate Icing

250g (8oz/1 cup) sugar
125ml (4fl oz/½ cup) water
150g (5oz) plain (semisweet)
chocolate, chopped
15ml (1 tablespoon) unflavoured
vegetable oil

In a medium-sized heavy-based
saucepan, heat the sugar in the
water until sugar has dissolved.
Boil rapidly until the syrup
reaches the thread stage (101°C/
215°F), and set aside. Melt the
chocolate and oil in a bowl over a
pan of hot water. Remove bowl
from pan and gradually add sugar
syrup to melted chocolate mixture, stirring until smooth. Cool
slightly before spreading on the
cold cake.

Chocolate Buttercream

60g (2oz/¼ cup) unsalted butter
300g (10oz/2½ cups) icing
(confectioner's) sugar, sifted
60g (2oz) plain or unsweetened
chocolate, melted and slightly
cooled
milk

Cream the butter until light and
very soft. Gradually add the sifted
sugar, creaming well after each
addition. Beat in the cooled
chocolate. The buttercream
should be very smooth. If it is too
stiff, add a little milk and beat
well.

Sachertorte

125g (4oz/½ cup) butter,
softened
125g (4oz/¾ cup) icing
(confectioner's) sugar
5 egg yolks
125g (4oz) plain (semisweet/dark)
chocolate, melted and cooled
vanilla essence to taste
185g (6oz/1½ cups) plain flour
4 egg whites

Icing
500g (1lb) plain (semisweet)
chocolate
250ml (8fl oz/1 cup) thick cream

Preheat oven to 180°C (350°F/ Gas 4). Grease and flour a 24cm (9in) round cake pan. Cream the butter and sugar; beat in the egg yolks. Stir in the melted chocolate and the vanilla essence. Fold in the flour. Whip the egg whites until stiff but not dry and carefully fold into the chocolate mixture. Pour into prepared pan. Bake in preheated oven for about 50 minutes. Leave until cold.

For the icing, melt 300g (10oz) of the chocolate in a bowl over a pan of hot water. Pour 185ml (6fl oz/2⁄3 cup) of the cream into a small saucepan and bring to a boil. Add the hot cream to the chocolate and beat well. Cool. As the mixture cools, it will become thick. Beat well to a creamy texture, then spread over the cake. Leave to set. Melt the remaining chocolate, boil the remaining cream, and beat together. Pour the hot icing over the cake and quickly smooth over with a palette knife. Leave to set, then pipe Sacher with piping chocolate.

CHOCOLATE CURLS

Chocolate curls can be used to decorate cakes or desserts. They are the traditional decoration on a Black Forest Gateau. Pour the melted chocolate onto a marble slab or follow the method here. Handle the curls carefully, as they are fragile and melt easily.

Pour the melted chocolate onto greaseproof paper. Pick up and drop the paper several times, or spread the chocolate backwards and forwards with a palette knife until it just sets.

Use a sharp knife held at a 45° angle to the chocolate. Shave the chocolate off the surface with a shearing action. The chocolate will form curls. The thickness depends on the length of the shearing action and the angle of the knife. Make chocolate shavings in the same way, but let the chocolate set firmer.

BLACK FOREST GATEAU

Cake
140g (5½oz/⅔ cup) unsalted (sweet) butter
100g (4oz/1 cup) caster sugar
100g (4oz) plain (semisweet) chocolate, broken into small pieces
6 eggs, separated
40g (1½oz/⅓ cup) fresh white or brown breadcrumbs
100g (4oz/1 cup) ground almonds
40g (1½oz/⅓ cup) plain (all-purpose) flour
40g (1½oz/⅓ cup) icing (confectioner's) sugar

Filling and topping
1.2L (40fl oz/5 cups) thick cream
900g (2lb) black cherries, stoned
Chocolate curls to decorate

Preheat the oven to 170°C (325°F/Gas Mark 3). Grease and flour a 24cm (9in) deep round cake pan. Melt together the butter and caster sugar in a large bowl over a pan of hot water. Add the chocolate and stir until melted. Remove from the heat.

Add the egg yolks, one at a time, to the chocolate mixture, beating well after each addition, until light and fluffy. Mix together the breadcrumbs, ground almonds and flour, and fold into the chocolate mixture.

Whip the egg whites with the icing sugar in a large bowl until stiff. Lightly fold into the chocolate mixture.

Pour into the prepared pan. Bake for about 1 hour, or until firm on top. Leave until cold.

To make the filling, whip the cream until double in volume.

Cut through the cold cake twice to make three rounds of equal thickness. Using a palette knife, spread a layer of cream on the bottom round. Place some of the cherries on top, then cover with the second layer. Spread this layer with cream. Place the remaining layer on top and spread the rest of the cream on the top and sides of the cake.

Pipe rosettes of cream around the top of the cake and put a cherry in each one. Decorate with chocolate curls.

CUTOUTS

Simple designs can be made by making chocolate cutouts using biscuit, cookie or aspic cutters, or by cutting the chocolate with a sharp knife around a template.

Be sure that the chocolate is smooth and an even thickness without any air bubbles, or the cutouts will not look attractive and may break.

Pour melted chocolate onto greaseproof paper. Pick up and drop the paper a few times so that the chocolate runs level and any air bubbles break. Leave until it starts to set.

Use biscuit cutters to cut out the shapes. Press in firmly without twisting to make a clean cut. Leave to harden on greaseproof paper before using as decorations.

Plastic cookie cutters can be filled with melted chocolate to make different shapes. Use a teaspoon to fill the cutter, then place on a small bowl or glass until the chocolate is completely set. Turn out onto greaseproof paper.

A selection of chocolate decorations made with commercial biscuit cutters.

Make a standing Christmas tree from cutouts by cutting two shapes with a tree cutter. Cut one in half with a hot sharp knife. Attach the whole tree to a flat chocolate base using melted chocolate. Position each half tree and attach with more melted chocolate. Add silver dragées.

PETAL CAKE

Cover a sponge cake with chocolate buttercream. Roll the sides in
chocolate vermicelli. Make a petal
template by tracing around a
barquette mould, and cut 16

petals from almost set plain
chocolate. Position round the
cake and attach with chocolate
buttercream. Decorate with
crystallized mimosa balls.

CHOCOLATE CUTOUT BOXES

Pour melted chocolate onto greaseproof paper, spreading it in an even layer with a palette knife. Pick up and drop the paper several times to eliminate any air bubbles. When the chocolate has set, cut with a sharp knife into 4cm (1½in) squares. Assemble the boxes with a little melted chocolate. They can be filled with squares of cake, fresh fruit or mousse. Decorate with piped cream. Another way of making chocolate sheets is to pour melted chocolate into a shallow tin. Drop the tin on the table several times to break any air bubbles, then cut the boxes in the same way.

CUTOUT CHOCOLATE CASKET

This chocolate casket is made by cutting out nearly set melted chocolate. Fill with chocolates or with fruit. Use as a centrepiece or an unusual gift.

Template for a casket pattern.

Make the templates from cardboard. Pour melted chocolate onto grease-proof paper. Pick up and drop the paper several times to break any air bubbles, then leave until just set. Using a sharp knife, cut out all of the pieces.

To assemble, attach the two base pieces, then assemble the sides around the inner base. Attach with piped melted chocolate. Put the two lid pieces together. Decorate the box with piped white chocolate. Fill with chocolates, fruit or after-dinner mints.

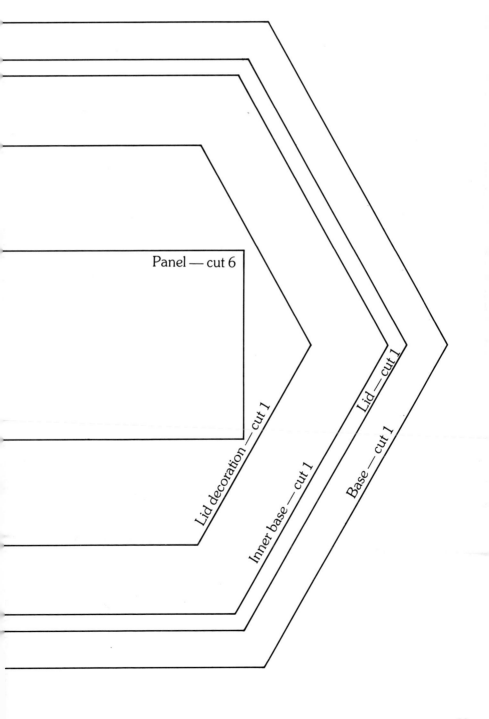

Panel — cut 6

Lid decoration — cut 1

Inner base — cut 1

Lid — cut 1

Base — cut 1

Lid — cut 1

CHOCOLATE LEAVES

Choose real leaves which have well-defined veins, such as those from roses, fuchsias or geraniums. Leave a bit of the stem to make handling easier. Clean with a damp cloth and dry thoroughly.

Use a medium-sized paintbrush to thickly coat the underside of each leaf with melted chocolate. Coat to the edge of the leaf, but do not go over the edge or it will be difficult to remove the leaf. Place on greaseproof paper to set, chocolate-side up. When the chocolate is firm, carefully peel the leaf away and place the chocolate leaf on greaseproof paper. Use the chocolate leaves to decorate cakes or desserts.

CHOCOLATE LEAF BIRTHDAY CAKE

Cover an oval cake with melted white chocolate and leave to set. Arrange the chocolate leaves on the cake. Pipe the chocolate stems. Make the plaque from a mould and overpipe with white chocolate.

CHOCOLATE CABBAGE

Choose a large cabbage with well defined veins and carefully peel the leaves away from the base. Place three small and three large leaves on the work surface with the cupped side upwards. Using a soup ladle, pour melted chocolate on the inside of the leaves. Take care not to let the chocolate run over the sides of the leaves or it will be difficult to peel them off.

Coat the leaves with chocolate three or four times. When set, carefully peel the cabbage leaves away. Dip the base of each leaf into melted chocolate and arrange around a centre of chocolate-covered swiss roll or scoops of ice cream.

To make a cabbage leaf dish for sweets or chocolates, pour melted chocolate on the outside of the leaf.

CHOCOLATE-DIPPED FRUIT

A chocolate fruit bowl filled with plain
and white chocolate-dipped fruit.

Fresh or crystallized fruit can be dipped
in chocolate. Choose small fruits such
as strawberries, grapes, raspberries
and cherries and dip them whole, or
use citrus fruit segments and pineapple
chunks. Wash and dry the fruit. Dip
into melted chocolate. Hold' over the
pan to let any excess chocolate drip
off, then leave to dry on greaseproof
paper. Dip a second time, if necessary,
and leave to set before serving.

For a chocolate strawberry dessert, fill
half a chocolate Easter egg with
chocolate-dipped strawberries. Decorate with chocolate rose leaves.

RUN OUTS

Choose pictures from children's books or colouring books, or draw your own. Place the design under wax paper. Melt the chocolate and pour into a piping bag. Do not let the chocolate get too hot or it will overflow to the outside of the design. Cut off the tip. Make a very small hole for a small design; for a larger design, cut the tip to represent a No1 or 2 nozzle. Pipe the design carefully. For a figure, pipe the body from side to side. For an arm, start at the top and run the chocolate down towards the hand. When the run outs are set, slip a small palette knife underneath and carefully lift off the wax paper.

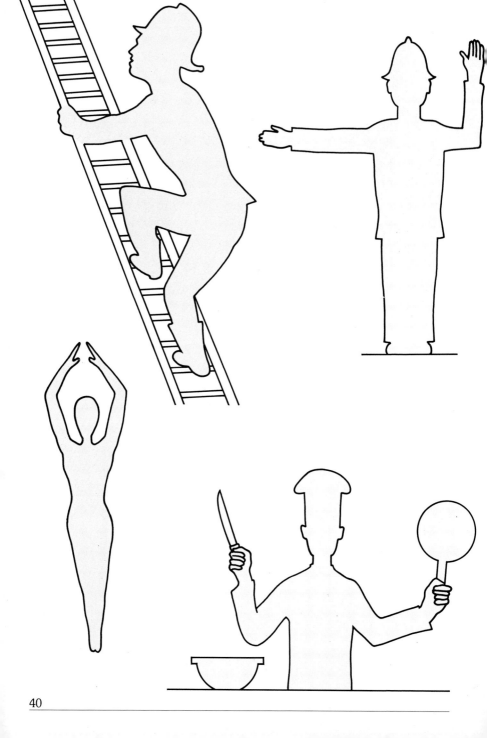

CHOCOLATE RICE PAPER

Rice paper cutouts can be dipped into melted chocolate to make unusual decorations. The main advantage of this technique is that it is possible to make shapes which are more intricate and delicate than those made by cutting melted chocolate with a knife or cutters.

Place the design on the table and put the rice paper over it with the shiny side up. Outline the design using a pen with edible ink. Leave a tab of rice paper at the widest point of the design, as shown on the templates. Cut out the design with scissors.

Hold the rice paper by the tab and dip in the melted chocolate. Allow any excess chocolate to drip off, then place the shape on a piece of greaseproof paper to dry. A single dipping is sufficient for a design to lie flat, but if the shape is to stand up, dip it a second time.

When the shape is completely dry, cut off the tab with scissors. Dip the end where the rice paper shows and leave to dry. For a standing figure, place the dipped end on the place where it is to stand and count to ten for it to harden off.

If the finished shape is to be curved, place it to dry on a piece of greaseproof paper in an apple

Three Kings

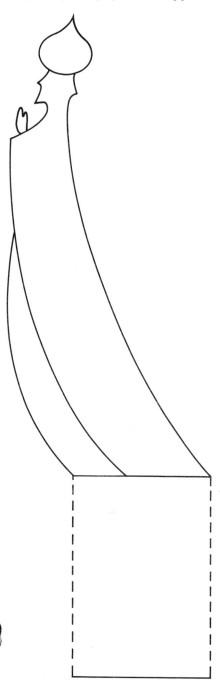

tray or cut a washing-up liquid bottle in half and dry on the curved side.

To make the turbans on the three kings, marble together some white and dark chocolate, then dip just the heads in this when the first coats have dried. This could be done for any parts of figures which need to be three-dimensional.

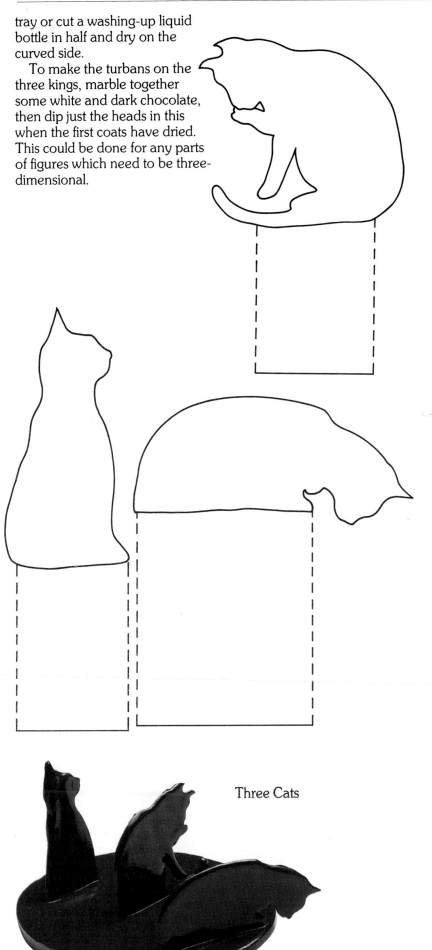

Three Cats

TRAIN CAKE

For the main part of the train, coat a swiss roll with melted chocolate. Place four large circles on a cake board and attach the train. Cut six small wheels and two large ones, and position. Make the chimney with five circles in front and three behind.

Cut the sides and roof of the cab from rice paper, following templates. Leave tabs, dip in chocolate and leave to set on greaseproof paper. Cut off tabs.

Attach to the train with melted chocolate.

For the face, cut a circle of sugarpaste with a fluted cutter. While the paste is soft, indent for the eyes. Royal ice the eyes. Attach a ball for the nose and another ball for the mouth. To open the mouth, insert a cocktail stick and rock it up and down. Pipe the hair. When the face is dry, attach to the front of the train with melted chocolate.

BUTTERCREAM CAKE WITH LILY

Coat a small round sponge cake with buttercream. Pipe the side decorations onto wax paper, then lift off and attach to the cake. The lily is made by dipping rice paper petals into melted chocolate. Make 12 petals by tracing round a barquette mould and dry over dowelling. Attach to the cake with buttercream.

BIRD HOUSE

Using the templates, cut the base, back and front and sides of the bird house. To make the entrance hole, dip a small round cutter in boiling water, wipe dry, then cut by pressing it in the chocolate and turning at the same time.

Make the roof tiles by cutting rice paper according to the template and dipping into melted chocolate. Assemble the pieces when the chocolate is dry and attach with piped melted chocolate.

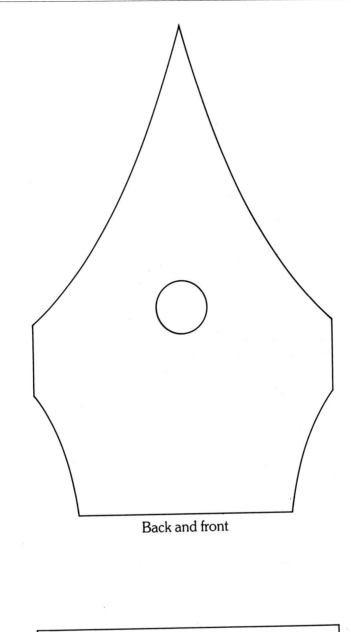

Back and front

Sides

Roof pieces

Boy and girl

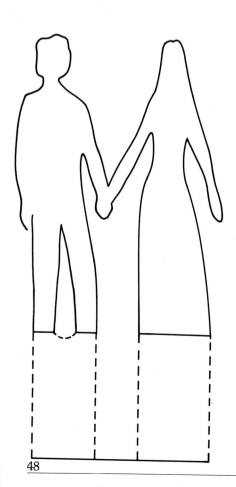
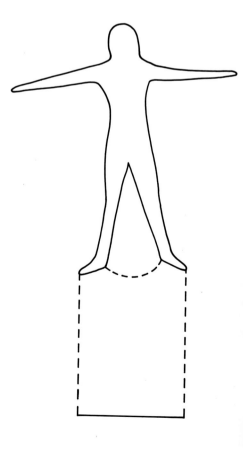

Keep-fit class

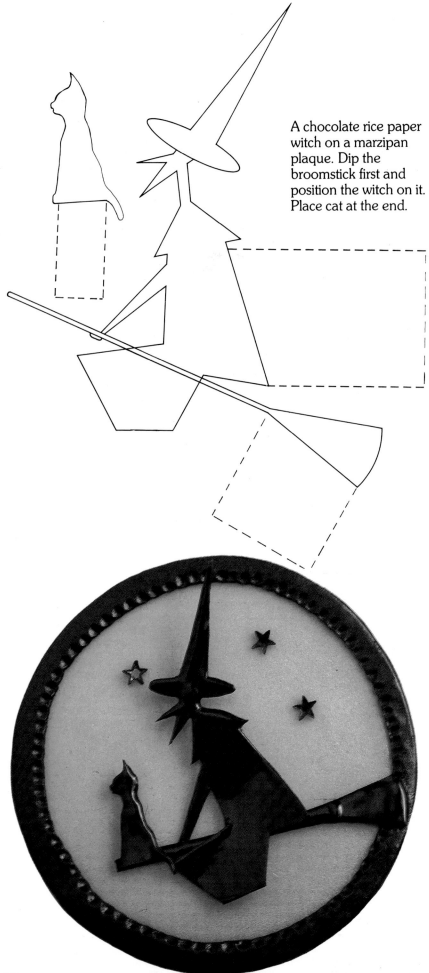

A chocolate rice paper witch on a marzipan plaque. Dip the broomstick first and position the witch on it. Place cat at the end.

CHOCOLATE ENGRAVING

Melt dark chocolate and use a paintbrush to paint a very thin, even layer on a baking tin. Brush one way, then the other way to get an even texture. Leave to dry. When the dark chocolate has set, pour on a layer of white or pastel-coloured chocolate about 3mm (⅛in) thick. When this is just set, cut out the plaque with a large cutter. Use the cutter to pick up the plaque and turn it over, ready for engraving. Choose a picture and transfer it to the plaque with a stylus, needle or hat pin. Engrave the plaque by scraping away the outline with a craft knife or scriber. Use a soft paintbrush to brush away the chocolate shavings as you work.

COCOA PAINTING

Cocoa painting can be done on plaques made of run-out royal icing, sugarpaste, rice paper, or pastillage. Trace the design onto the plaque. Melt a small amount of cocoa butter in an egg poacher or a small double saucepan. Do not let it get too hot, as it will be ruined if it is allowed to boil. If cocoa butter is unavailable, use white fat or shortening, although the results may not be as good. Put some cocoa powder at the side of the melted cocoa butter and use a paintbrush to mix to the desired shade of brown. Use brushes of different thicknesses for the painting. Outline the design first. If painting a landscape, start at the background and work forward. Shading improves the picture. Clean the brushes by dipping them in the melted cocoa butter and wiping on kitchen paper.

MAKING PIPING BAGS

Piping chocolate

To prepare chocolate for piping, melt 125g (4oz) and add two or three drops of glycerine to thicken it. The chocolate can also be thickened with piping jelly, spirits or liqueurs.

Cut a piece of greaseproof paper twice as long as it is wide.

Fold the paper diagonally.
The points will not meet.

Cut along the fold with a sharp knife to
make two right-angle triangles.

Lay the triangle flat with the right angle
facing you and fold the corner inwards.

Place the corner on the point of the
right angle, making a cone.

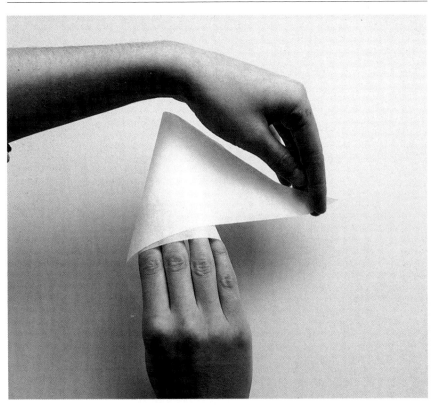

Put your fingers in the cone to hold it
and bring the other corner over it.

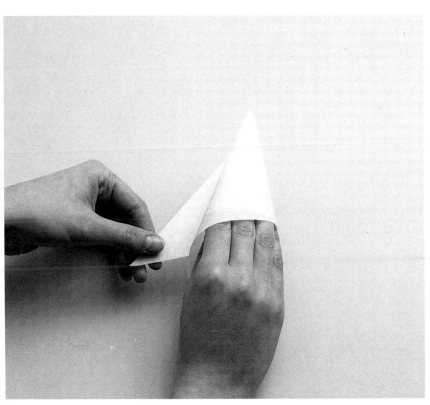

Wrap the corner around the cone
twice so that the point goes over top.

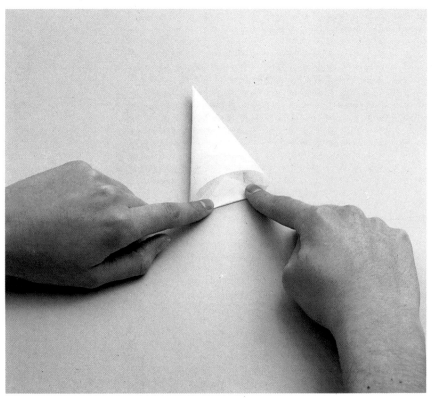

Slide the three points together to
tighten the bag, or, to make a narrow
bag, bring the top point over, tuck it in,
fold over, make two small tears to lock
it in position.

Fold the top point into the bag. Fill,
then fold in the corners towards the
centre and fold over the top to secure.
Cut off the tip to pipe.

LETTERING

Chocolate lettering needs to be flowing, as it is more difficult to stop and restart when piping with chocolate than it is with royal icing. Pour the piping chocolate into a small piping bag and cut off the tip. Do not use a tube, as the chocolate sets quickly and will harden in the tube. Pipe the lettering onto a cake or plaque, or onto greaseproof paper and remove when set.

With Love

Happy Birthday

Easter Greetings

On your Retirement

Congratulations

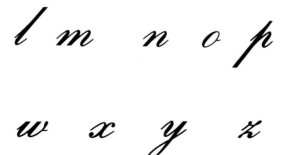

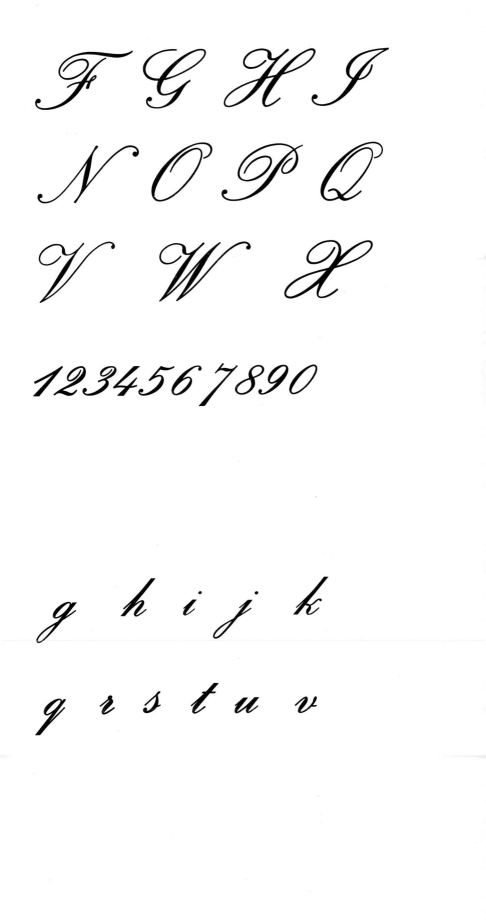

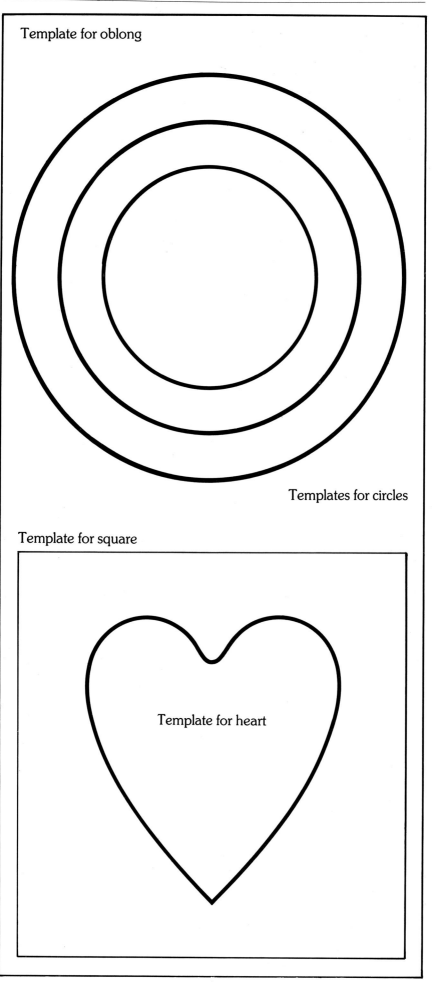

Template for oblong

Templates for circles

Template for square

Template for heart

PIPED SCROLLS AND SHELLS

To pipe chocolate scrolls or shells onto a cake, use a No7 or No43 star or shell tube in a medium-sized bag. Fill a bag with piping chocolate and pipe the design onto the cake.

TUBE EMBROIDERY

Chocolate embroidery can be very effective on sweets or to decorate a cake. Any chocolate can be used, although coloured white chocolate is most attractive. Pipe the design freehand, or scratch it into the surface using a scriber or hat pin.

Fill a small piping bag with the melted chocolate and cut off the tip to represent a No0 or 1 tube. Pipe the design, working with one colour at a time. Leave to dry.

Moulded chocolate Easter eggs decorated with piped chocolate embroidery.

BRUSH EMBROIDERY

Chocolate brush embroidery can be used on chocolate plaques or Easter eggs, or brushed directly onto a cake. Coloured white chocolate is most effective. Work freehand, or scratch the design onto the surface using a scriber or a hat pin. Fill a small bag with un-thickened chocolate and cut off the tip. Pipe the outline, then quickly brush towards the centre with a fine paintbrush. Work on a small section at a time, such as a single petal or leaf, and work quickly, as the chocolate becomes unworkable as it sets. When the brush embroidery is dry, pipe in any details such as veins or stems.

A simple plaque for a Christmas cake featuring a brush embroidered Christmas rose and ivy.

A white chocolate plaque with brush embroidered rose piped with pastel-coloured white chocolate.

Chocolate Easter eggs decorated with brush embroidered flowers.

FILIGREE AND LACE

Piped chocolate lace or filigree pieces, also called off-pieces, can be used to decorate cakes or sweets. Place the design under wax paper. Fill a bag with piping chocolate and cut off the tip to represent a No1 tube. Pipe the design. When set, slide a thin palette knife under each piece to release it.

Off-piece for Lily cake.

A selection of chocolate lace and filigree.

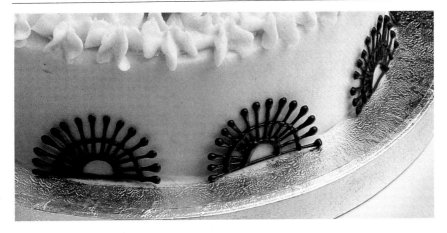

FREESTANDING FILIGREE ORNAMENTS

Christmas tree

Centrepiece

Place the design under wax paper. Score round the design with a fingernail so that the wax paper sticks to it.

Melt 125g (4oz) couverture and add two or three drops of glycerine to it. Pour some into a piping bag without a nozzle and cut off the end for a No1 tube. Pipe the four pieces of the ornament. When the chocolate is completely set, release from the wax paper by gently working from the wide end. Turn over and pipe the other side for greater strength.

To assemble, lay a left-hand and right-hand piece on a piece of wax paper and attach by piping melted chocolate down the centre. Fix the third side in the centre with melted chocolate, supporting gently. Count to ten to allow the chocolate to set.

With your fingertips, carefully lift the ornament upright. Fix the fourth side with melted chocolate and count to ten for it to set.

The filigree ornament can be placed on a cake, on a thin cake board or on a cut or moulded chocolate base. Attach in the centre with melted chocolate.

Christmas tree:
pipe four halves

Base for Christmas tree

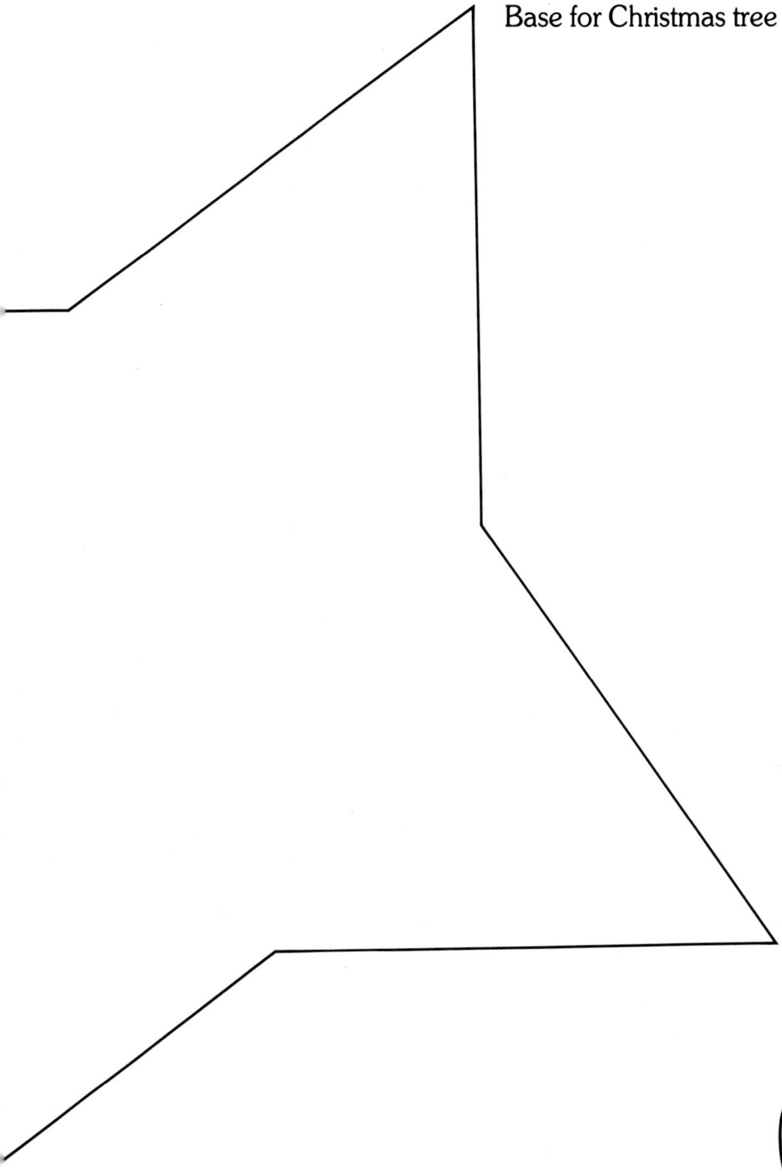

Centrepiece:
pipe four

FILIGREE SWAN BOX

For the base, trace the outline of the template for the top and cut out the shape from melted chocolate which has nearly set. Trace the design for the top and four pieces for the sides, and place under wax paper. Pipe the pieces using piping chocolate in a piping bag cut to a No1 tube. When the filigree has set, carefully release each piece from the wax paper. Turn them over and pipe on the reverse side for extra strength. To assemble, position the sides on the base and attach with piped chocolate. Leave to set. Pipe chocolate around the top edges and carefully position the top of the box.

Top and base

Sides: pipe four

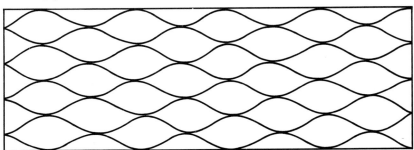

CHOCOLATE HOT-AIR BALLOON

Blow up a 22cm (9in) round balloon, tie it and spray it with cocoa butter. Leave to dry, then spray it again. Place in a 10cm (4in) ring, such as a cardboard tube, or a bowl.

Melt couverture in the usual way and add glycerine to make piping chocolate. Baker's chocolate cannot be used because the fat content from the cocoa butter would make it too soft to hold the shape.

Fill a piping bag and begin by piping a circle around the top of the balloon. Pipe drop loops around the edge, and continue in this way until halfway down. Leave to set, then turn upsidedown. Leave a section uncovered to fit in the base, then pipe exactly as before until the two piped sections meet.

Pipe four lines curved at the bottom where the balloon has been tied. Leave until the chocolate is completely set. Release the balloon from the chocolate by pressing in with the hairs of a paintbrush. If a section does not come away, leave until it is firmer. Untie the knot and release the air slowly.

The basket base is made from a 5cm (2in) square chocolate cutout. Cut four supports 1 x 8cm (¼ x 3½in), and a ring with a 6.5cm (2½in) outside diameter and a 5cm (2in) inside diameter. Leave until firm.

To make the basketwork on the four sides, place wax paper over a 5cm (2in) square template. Pipe diagonal lines 3mm (⅛in) apart first in one direction, then in the opposite direction. Finish off the sides with a snailstrail. Attach the sides to the base with melted chocolate. Dip the four supports in melted chocolate and place one in each corner of the basket. Put a blob of melted chocolate on each support and fit the ring on top. Make a marzipan animal balloonist and position in the basket. The balloon should fit snugly into the ring and should not need to be fixed.

MODELLING WITH CHOCOLATE

This chocolate modelling compound can be used to make moulded flowers and figures. It is easy to work with and does not require any adhesives, as the moulded pieces will stick to each other. If there are any cracks, smooth over them with your finger. The modelling compound will keep for several weeks without refrigeration. Wrap it in cling film and place in a plastic container stored in a cool place. When ready to work with the paste, cut off a piece and knead. Take care not to over-knead or the ingredients will separate. If it becomes too soft, put in a cool place until it becomes firm.

> **Chocolate modelling compound**
> 125g (5oz) baker's chocolate
> 100ml (4fl oz/½ cup) liquid glucose or corn syrup
> Melt the chocolate in a double saucepan. Warm the liquid glucose or corn syrup and mix well with the chocolate. Wrap in cling film, place in a plastic bag or container, and leave to set for at least one hour before modelling.

TEDDY BEAR

For the body, make a cone with 20g (⅔oz) and flatten the top slightly for the head.

For the legs, make a sausage with 5g (⅙oz). Indent with the little finger. Cut in half lengthwise, turn up the feet and attach legs to body. Mark claws with the back of a knife. Use 2g (¹⁄₁₅oz) for both arms and make as for legs.

For the head, make a cone with 10g (⅓oz). Cut mouth with a sharp knife, place the knife point inside and press down to open. Squeeze sides of the mouth to make a smile. Make indentations with a ball tool for the eye sockets. For the ears, make two tiny balls and attach to the top of the head. Place a finger behind each ear for support and make indentations with a ball tool. Pipe eyes.

ROSE

For the stand, make a cone with modelling compound. One-third of the way up, indent by gently rolling between the outside of your little fingers. Position the first petal on the cone as shown. Place the second petal opposite the first.

Roll out the modelling compound very thinly and cut with a rose petal cutter.

Place three more petals interlocking using the edge of the second petal as the centre line of the third petal. At this stage it is called a half rose.

If adding more petals, cut them with the next larger sized petal cutter. Fix them lower than the first layer and curl back the edges.

Cut leaves using a leaf cutter or a template.

CAT

For the body, make a cone with 15g (½oz).

Attach a long, tapered sausage for the tail.

Make a 5g (⅙oz) ball for the head. Gently pinch up ears and indent with a ball tool. Make indentations for eyes and pipe. Mark whiskers with a knife. Add small nose and mouth.

CHICK

For the body, make a ball with 15g (½oz) modelling compound. Indent the centre for the head to sit.

Head is a 5g (⅙oz) ball. Make indentations for the eyes. Cut the mouth. Pipe eyes.

Make a cone for the tail and flatten it. Snip the feathers with scissors. Make two smaller cones for the wings and snip the feathers.

SCOTTIE DOG

For the body, cut the 15g (½oz) sausage at both ends for the legs. Bend to shape. Snip the tail with scissors.

Make a long sausage with 20g (⅔oz) and cut off one quarter (5g (⅙oz)) for the head. Pinch up the ears and indent with a ball tool. Pinch out sides and snip for whiskers. Indent eyes with a ball tool. Indent for nose and mouth with a cocktail stick, then position small round balls. Pipe eyes.

DACHSHUND

For the body, make a sausage with 15g (½oz) of modelling compound. Make a tiny cone, flatten it and attach the fat side to the body for the tail.

Make four tiny sausages for the feet and position under the body.

The head is a 5g (⅙oz) cone. Indent the eyes with a ball tool, and position a small oval nose. Make two flattened cones for the ears and position on the sides of the head. Pipe eyes.

EASTER EGG HOUSE

Large chocolate Easter eggs decorated with marzipan. Add marzipan rabbits and attach to a large cake board. Finish off with chocolate and sugar Easter eggs, foil-wrapped chocolate coins and arrange rice paper washing on a line.

MOULDING HOLLOW SHAPES

The Easter eggs and hollow chocolate figures on the following pages are all made by the method shown here. Choose any of the many plastic or metal moulds available from specialist shops or department stores.

Melt the chocolate in the usual way. The mould should be clean and dry. Polish over the inside surface with cotton wool.

Using a large wooden spoon or a soup ladle, fill the mould with melted chocolate and level the top with a palette knife. Place in a small bowl to keep the mould upright and leave in a cool place until the chocolate sets around the edge. For a thicker rim, leave to set longer.

Pour off the excess chocolate and turn the mould upside-down on a piece of greaseproof paper. Repeat Step 2 if necessary, to make a thicker chocolate coating. Two layers should be sufficient for most eggs and figures.

When the desired thickness is reached, place the mould in a cool place until the chocolate is completely set. If unmoulded too soon, the chocolate will crack or break.

To unmould, turn out on a piece of greaseproof paper or on the work surface. The chocolate should come out of the mould easily; if it does not, return the mould to a cool place and allow to harden further. To join the two halves of an Easter egg or figure, briefly place one half on a heated baking tray and quickly press on the other half.

89

EASTER EGGS

An egg made with peach-tinted white chocolate and decorated with chocolate moulded flowers. Pipe the stems and embroidery with coloured white chocolate.

Make three eggs for the carriages and a larger egg for the engine. Cut out the doors by dipping a cutter in hot water, drying, then cutting by pressing in and twisting. Trim with coloured marzipan. The wheels are circles cut from melted chocolate. Mould a chimney from marzipan or chocolate modelling compound.

Make an egg for the base of the helicopter. Cut the door by dipping a cutter in hot water, drying, and then cutting by pressing in and twisting. Trim with marzipan. Cut circles from melted chocolate for the base, stairs, wheels and top. The blades are made by dipping rice paper strips into melted chocolate. Add a marzipan chick.

A selection of eggs decorated with flowers and ribbons. The bases are made from chocolate shells.

Make a chocolate egg for the base of the cradle. Take the wide part of a second egg and attach for the hood. Decorate with marzipan. Add a marzipan rabbit baby and cover with a blanket made from marzipan pressed on a nutmeg grater for texture.

SWAN WITH FILIGREE WINGS

Make the swan from a mould. Pipe the filigree wings using a bag cut to a No1 tube and filled with piping chocolate. Pipe different-sized pieces freehand. When dry, carefully remove the wings from the wax paper and position on the swan with melted chocolate. Tie a narrow ribbon around the swan's neck.

LARGE CHOCOLATE MOULDS

To make chocolate figures with white insets, prepare the moulds as usual. Fill the areas to be white with melted white chocolate and leave in a cool place to set completely. Mould the dark chocolate in the usual way. This technique can also be used with coloured white chocolate.

A plain chocolate owl made from a traditional mould.

A rabbit pulling a cart filled with sugar Easter eggs. Use a heated cutter to cut out the top of the cart after the two pieces are stuck together.

A white chocolate moulded snowman wearing a red marzipan scarf. Pipe the broom from milk chocolate.

CHOCOLATE BOWLS

Chocolate bowls can be made from any bowl, but metal or plastic ones are the easiest to use because they contract and expand with temperature changes. Choose a bowl with an interesting shape, and one which has a smooth, even surface with no chips, cracks or scratches. Polish with cotton wool.

Fill the bowl with melted chocolate. Leave until the chocolate sets around the rim, then pour out the excess. If a thicker coating is required leave to set longer. Turn out when the chocolate is completely set.

Alternatively, coat the outside of the bowl with melted chocolate and leave to set upsidedown on greaseproof paper. Coat several times. Carefully remove the chocolate shell when it has set completely.

A chocolate bowl filled with chocolate-dipped fresh fruit. The base of the bowl is a candy dish moulded in the same way.

This bowl has been decorated with moulded white chocolate cameo figures and piped dropped loops. Turn the bowl upsidedown, support on a tin or similar object, and pipe the loops freehand. Dry for a few minutes, then turn right-side up.

MOULDING SMALL SHAPES

Small solid eggs and chocolates are very easy to make. Polish the moulds with cotton wool and place on the work surface. Melt the chocolate in the normal way. Fill the moulds to the top by piping in the melted chocolate, or use a chocolate funnel or a teaspoon. Level off the tops and place in a cool place until set. The chocolate will contract away from the sides of the moulds when firm.

Turn out the chocolates onto the work surface or greaseproof paper. If joining together two shapes, such as the halves of an Easter egg, either pipe a ring of chocolate and press the two halves together, or briefly put one half on a heated baking tray and quickly press on the other half.

Make the basket from a basket mould and place on a thin cake board. Trim with marzipan and fill with an assortment of solid chocolate Easter eggs and marzipan eggs.

COLOURING WHITE CHOCOLATE

White chocolate can be coloured before moulding to give an interesting effect to the finished chocolates. For best results, use petal dust or oil-based food colouring made for chocolate work. Do not add liquid food colouring, which will thicken the chocolate and make it impossible to mould. Coloured chocolate can also be used for any decorative work.

Melt the white chocolate. If making coloured chocolates, choose moulds, such as cameos, which are well defined and will show up the different colours.

Put some chocolate in a small bowl. Add some petal dust and mix well with a palette knife. Start with a very small amount of colouring and add more if a darker shade is required.

If making plain coloured chocolates, fill the moulds with the coloured chocolate and leave to set. To make the flower cameos, fill piping bags and pipe the outlines of the flowers and leaves in coloured chocolate. Leave to set.

For the cameos, fill the moulds to the top with white or plain chocolate and leave in a cool place to set. Turn out of the moulds when the chocolate is firm.

MARBLED CHOCOLATES

To make the marbled shells, fill the moulds with melted white chocolate. Pour in a very small amount of melted plain chocolate and quickly swirl through with a cocktail stick. The smaller shapes are made by filling the moulds with plain chocolate and swirling through a tiny amount of white chocolate.

LAYERED COLOURED CHOCOLATES

Although any mould can be used, the geometric shapes shown here work best, as the layers are clearly shown. Use layers of plain, white and milk chocolate, or three different colours of white chocolate. Polish the moulds with cotton wool, then pour in the first layer and put in a cool place to set. Add the second and third layers, taking care that each colour is dry and set before pouring in the next one. Turn out the finished chocolates.

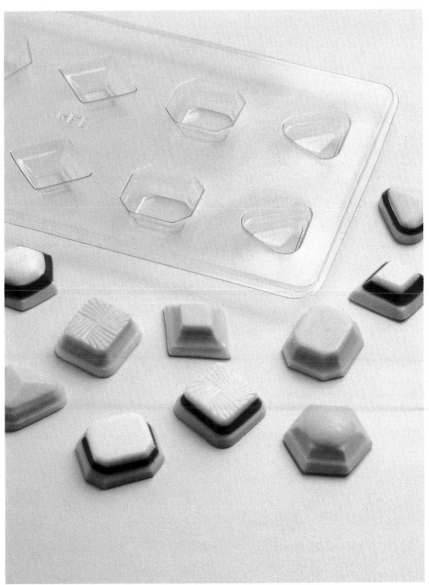

CHOCOLATE CONES

Make a piping bag from grease-proof paper and tape the seam. Insert a small plastic container and hold the flap of the bag against the container with your forefinger. Pour a thick coating of chocolate over the bag. When it is completely covered, place it on a board to set.

If a cone with a smooth finish is desired, carefully remove the container and piping bag now. To remove the piping bag, first peel the edge away from the sides of the cone. Twist the bag between your fingers and gently pull it away from the chocolate.

If you want a cone with a log appearance, use a thick paintbrush to stipple on more chocolate. Leave to set.

A smooth-finish cone made with a cream horn mould and filled with marbled shells.

CAMEO MOULDS

There are several different types of cameo moulds available. Polish the mould with cotton wool and fill with melted chocolate. Because the cameo shapes are very shallow, it is easiest to fill them using a small piping bag. If wished, make the shapes in one colour of chocolate and the oval background pieces in a contrasting colour.

Leave in a cool place until completely set, then turn out the chocolates. The shapes can be attached to a box or bowl, as shown, or position the figures on the oval backgrounds.

SMALL CHOCOLATES MADE FROM MOULDS

Plain chocolates with white chocolate insets. Pipe in the white chocolate and allow to set completely before filling the moulds with plain chocolate.

To make chocolate lollies, choose fairly large plastic moulds. Pipe in the white chocolate and leave to set. Fill the moulds with milk or plain chocolate, position a lolly stick, and put in a cool place until hard before turning out.

Make chocolate mice by filling plastic moulds with coloured white chocolate. Add a string tail, and leave the moulds in a cool place until completely firm. Turn out and pipe the eyes in a contrasting colour chocolate.

A simple way of making chocolate Christmas tree ornaments is to fill any mould with chocolate and place a loop of ribbon in the slightly set chocolate. Leave in a cool place until completely firm, then turn out.

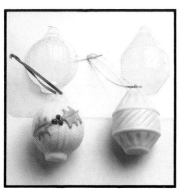

Special moulds are available to make chocolate Christmas tree ornaments. Simply fill with any colour chocolate and leave until set. Join the two halves by placing one half on a heated baking tray and then quickly pressing on the other. Decorate with piped chocolate, if wished. Use a hot darning needle to make a hole in the top and thread a ribbon through.

CHOCOLATE BOXES

To make chocolate boxes, use one of the commercial plastic moulds available. Polish the base and lid with cotton wool, then fill both parts with melted chocolate. Leave in a cool place until the chocolate begins to set around the edge, then pour off the excess chocolate. Leave in a cool place until the chocolate is firm, then fill again. An average-sized box will need three or four coats. When the chocolate is completely set, turn out of the mould. Another method is to leave the chocolate in the mould until a ridge appears around the edge before pouring off the surplus. Only one coat of chocolate will be needed. Fill the box with chocolates.

A white chocolate heart trimmed with piped chocolate and moulded holly leaves and berries.

Another white chocolate box decorated with moulded chocolate roses.

Plain and milk chocolate heart boxes decorated with moulded chocolate roses.

CHOCOLATE CAKE CASES

Put together two paper cake cases. Pour in melted chocolate to fill. Leave in a cool place until a ridge appears around the surface, then pour off any excess. Leave until the chocolate shell is completely set, then peel away the paper. Fill the cases with cake, ice cream or fruit and decorate with piped cream and grated chocolate.

Cake or sweet cases can also be made using small paper or foil sweet cases.

CHOCOLATE BOATS

Make the boats by filling small metal barquette moulds with melted chocolate. Put in a cool place until firm, then turn out.

The oars are marzipan sausages dipped in chocolate. Add marzipan animals and decorate with paper umbrellas.

TRUFFLES

Chocolate truffles

125g (4oz) plain (semisweet) or
milk chocolate, chopped
30ml (2 tablespoons) cream,
lightly whipped
15ml (1 tablespoon) rum or
sherry
125-150g (4-5oz/1-1¼ cups)
icing (confectioner's) sugar, sifted
chocolate vermicelli (sprinkles) or
cocoa powder

Melt the chocolate in a bowl over
a pan of hot water. Remove bowl
from pan and stir in cream and
rum or sherry. Add enough sugar
to make a soft paste. Cover and
refrigerate for 1 hour. Form into
small balls and roll in chocolate
vermicelli or cocoa powder.

Party favours: Make the
white chocolate dishes
from moulds, or use tiny
china or glass bowls or
clean seashells. Place a

White chocolate truffles

125g (4oz) white dessert chocolate
125g (4oz/½ cup) unsalted butter
125g (4oz/1 cup) icing (confectioner's) sugar, sifted
15ml (1 tablespoon) brandy
dessicated (shredded) coconut (optional)

Melt the chocolate in a bowl over a pan of hot water. Leave to cool slightly. Cream together the butter and icing sugar until very light and fluffy. Beat in the cooled white chocolate and the brandy. Refrigerate for 1 hour. Roll into small balls, and roll in the dessicated coconut, if wished.

plain, milk and white chocolate truffle in each dish, and use as individual favours or place markers.

TRUFFLES

Christmas pudding truffles: Make chocolate truffles and dust them with cocoa powder. Make the plates from marzipan cut to shape with a fluted cutter. Leave to dry in a curved shape overnight, then attach the truffles with a little melted chocolate. Pour melted white chocolate over each one and decorate with tiny marzipan holly leaves and berries.

Truffle tree: Turn an ice cream cone upside-down so that the wide part forms the base of the tree. Pour melted chocolate over the cone to completely cover it. Build up the tree from the base, starting with larger truffles. Dip each one in melted chocolate and attach to the base. If the truffles have been dipped in cocoa powder, wipe some away or they will not stick to the base. Use plain, milk and white chocolate truffles, arranging them in a pattern with the smaller truffles at the top of the tree.

Christmas wreath: Draw a circle on a board or on a sugarpasted cake. Arrange the truffles around the outline. Add chocolate holly leaves made from real leaves or from moulds. Finish with a chocolate run out bow, or add a ribbon bow.

FONDANTS

Fondant centres are one of the most popular fillings for chocolates. Purchased melting fondant is often smoother and easier to work with than homemade fondant, and is available from cake decorating suppliers and other specialist shops.

To make fondant centres, heat 450g (1lb) fondant in a double saucepan. When melted, add 15ml (3 teaspoons) invert sugar or honey and enough water or stock syrup to get a smooth, flowing consistency. Continue stirring until the fondant reaches 49°C (120°F), when it will be liquid enough to pour.

Colour the fondant with paste colours, and flavour with essences, oil or concentrated fruit juices. Mix each fondant in a small bowl, and work with one at a time, as it sets quickly.

Fondant

900g (2lb/4 cups) preserving (lump) sugar
300ml (10fl oz/1¼ cups) water
pinch of cream of tartar dispersed in a few drops of water

Dissolve the sugar in the water in a large, heavy-based saucepan. Heat to a temperature of 107°C (225°F). Pour in the cream of tartar solution and continue heating. Do not stir, but wash down the sides of the pan occasionally to prevent premature crystallization. Bring to a temperature of 115°C (240°F), then remove from the heat.

Have ready a frame made from metal bars positioned on a marble slab. Moisten the marble with cold water, then pour in the fondant. Splash with cold water. Leave until the temperature is 39°C (100°F). Remove the frame and knead the fondant mixture. It will turn opaque, then white. Knead until it is firm and very white.

Place in a bowl and cover with a thin layer of water to prevent a crust forming. Leave overnight before using.

Fondant centres

	colour	flavour
Rose creams	pink	rose water
Violet creams	lilac or violet	violet essence or oil
Orange	orange	orange oil or concentrated juice, plus finely grated rind
Lemon	yellow	lemon oil or juice, plus finely grated rind
Coffee	brown	coffee essence, or 5ml (1 teaspoon) double strength coffee
Mint	green	peppermint oil

Assemble all the equipment before starting. Fondant sets quickly, so make double piping bags and prepare the starch tray before heating the fondant in the double saucepan.

Made indentations in the starch tray using chocolate moulds, the end of a wooden rolling pin, or the back of a knife.

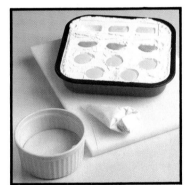

Fill a piping bag with the coloured and flavoured fondant and quickly pipe into the shapes. Use small bags and work quickly. Put the tray in a cool place and leave to set.

Remove the fondants from the starch tray after about three hours. They should still be slightly soft, but firm enough to handle. Place on silicone or greaseproof paper and leave to harden overnight. Brush off any cornflour with a pastry brush before dipping in chocolate.

Starch tray

Fondants can be made with a starch tray which allows the centres to dry out while still keeping their shapes. Use a metal baking tin about 4cm (1½in) deep, and fill with sifted, dry, warm cornflour (cornstarch). Level the top with a metal ruler. Make indentations for the fondant using a wooden stick, knife handle or chocolate moulds, leaving about 2cm (¾in) between each indentation to prevent the cornflour from caving in. The cornflour can be reused several times, but must be dried and resifted into the tray each time.

DIPPED CHOCOLATES

Hand-dipped chocolates are impressive and easy to make. Use fondant centres, or dip cherries, nuts, marzipan, candied or crystallized fruit, or sugarpaste cut into shapes with small cutters.

Milk, plain or white chocolate are all suitable for hand dipping. Although couverture will give a better flavour and snap, baker's chocolate will also give good results.

CENTRES FOR DIPPING

Gianduja

250g (8oz) plain (semisweet) chocolate, melted
250g (8oz/1 cup) hazelnut-chocolate spread
375-500g (12-16oz/3-4 cups) mixed chopped nuts and candied cherries

Mix together the melted chocolate and hazelnut-chocolate spread. Stir in the chopped nuts and cherries. Pour into a 2.5-4cm (1-1½in) deep tin which has been lined with baking (parchment) paper. Leave to set overnight, then cut into 2cm (¾in) squares, and dip in chocolate.

Citrus and honey centre

30ml (2 tablespoons) frozen orange juice concentrate
125g (4oz/½ cup) honey
90g (3oz/⅓ cup) hazelnut-chocolate spread
375g (12oz) plain (semisweet) chocolate, melted
180g (6oz/1½ cups) finely minced candied citrus peel

In a medium-sized saucepan, melt the orange juice concentrate, honey and hazelnut-chocolate spread. Stir in the melted chocolate. Add the minced peel and mix well. Pour into a 2.5-4cm (1-1½in) deep tin which has been lined with baking (parchment) paper. Leave to set overnight, then cut into 2cm (¾in) squares and dip in chocolate.

Assemble all the equipment before starting. The centres must be at room temperature. Melt the chocolate in a double saucepan. Special dipping forks for chocolate work are available, or use a carving fork or large table fork. Have ready several sheets of greaseproof paper on which to set the dipped chocolates.

Dip each centre individually. Place in the melted chocolate, then turn over using a fork so that it is completely coated. Tap the fork on the side of the pan to remove any excess chocolate, then place the chocolate on the paper and leave to set. Decorate with piped chocolate designs, crystallized fruit or flowers or chopped nuts.

DIPPED CHOCOLATES

After dinner mints made from mint-flavoured fondant and dipped in plain chocolate. Serve decorated with crystallized mint leaves.

Chocolate-covered sugarpaste cut in an assortment of shapes and dipped in milk and plain chocolate. Knead in colouring and flavouring before rolling out and cutting with small pastry or aspic cutters. Decorate with piped chocolate or crystallized flowers.

Dip hazelnuts in melted chocolate and form into clusters to set. Almonds, brazil nuts and candied cherries can all be dipped individually.

Marzipan dipped in plain chocolate. Cut squares of one colour, or make shapes using two different colours. Leave the top uncovered for a more interesting effect.

LIQUEUR CHOCOLATES

Liqueur chocolates are chocolate shells filled with a sugar syrup containing spirit or liqueur. Because of the expense involved in making these chocolates, it is worth using couverture rather than baker's chocolate to get a better flavour. Any spirit or liqueur can be used, although it may be necessary to change the amount of sugar used in the syrup if the liqueur contains a lot of sugar, which may crystallize too quickly.

Sugar syrup for liqueur chocolates

250g (8oz/1 cup) sugar
60ml (4 tablespoons) cold water
30ml (2 tablespoons) liqueur

Place the sugar and water in a small, heavy-based saucepan over high heat. Bring to a boil and dissolve the sugar. Have ready a bowl of cold water and a pastry brush to brush down the sides of the pan as the syrup boils to stop premature crystallization.

Boil until the syrup reaches 108°C (225°F/transparent icing) on a sugar thermometer.

Have ready a clean, dry and warmed preserving jar. If planning on making more than one kind of liqueur chocolate, prepare a jar for each one. When the syrup reaches the correct temperature, pour it in the jar. Add the liqueur and quickly seal the jar. Turn gently to mix.

Place the sealed jar in a bowl of tepid water. Gradually add ice to bring down the temperature of the syrup. It is ready for use when cold.

Assemble all the equipment before starting. A sugar thermometer is essential for liqueur chocolates. Choose chocolate moulds which are fairly deep for best results.

Polish the moulds with cotton wool. Pour in the tempered couverture, then tip out the excess to leave a thin layer of chocolate in the mould. Leave in a cool place to set.

Make the liqueur syrup following the recipe. Do not be tempted to add more than 30ml (2 tablespoons) of alcohol, or the syrup may crystallize.

Place the sealed jar in a bowl of tepid water, then add ice to bring the temperature down. The liqueur syrup must be completely cold before it is piped in the chocolate shells.

Make a double-thickness piping bag. Pour some syrup into the bag using a small soup ladle, then cut off the tip and quickly fill the chocolate shells to within 3mm (⅛in) of the top. Put in a cool place, but do not refrigerate, for about 24 hours. A thin film or crust of sugar will set over the surface.

Dip a palette knife in the chocolate and quickly go over the surface to seal in the syrup. Leave until set, then turn out of the moulds.

PACKAGING

Beautifully packaged homemade chocolates make wonderful presents. Buy small boxes or bags from stationers or sugarcraft suppliers, or save small boxes. Paper and foil sweet cases are available from supermarkets.

Truffles packed in a Continental-style chocolate box. Tie with ribbons and decorate with silk flowers.

An Easter egg in a colourful presentation box, tied with matching ribbons.

A transparent heart-shaped box decorated with a moulded chocolate rose and filled with chocolates.

Fill small foil bags with assorted chocolates and tie with matching ribbon.

An unusual box decorated with a chocolate run out Christmas rose and moulded chocolate holly leaves.

Tiny boxes which hold two chocolates make attractive place markers or party favours.